Put Beginning Readers on the Right Track with
ALL ABOARD READING™

The All Aboard Reading series is especially for beginning readers. Written by noted authors and illustrated in full color, these are books that children really and truly *want* to read—books to excite their imagination, tickle their funny bone, expand their interests, and support their feelings. With four different reading levels, All Aboard Reading lets you choose which books are most appropriate for your children and their growing abilities.

Picture Readers—for Ages 3 to 6
Picture Readers have super-simple texts, with many nouns appearing as rebus pictures. At the end of each book are 24 flash cards—on one side is the rebus picture; on the other side is the written-out word.

Level 1—for Preschool through First-Grade Children
Level 1 books have very few lines per page, very large type, easy words, lots of repetition, and pictures with visual "cues" to help children figure out the words on the page.

Level 2—for First-Grade to Third-Grade Children
Level 2 books are printed in slightly smaller type than Level 1 books. The stories are more complex, but there is still lots of repetition in the text, and many pictures. The sentences are quite simple and are broken up into short lines to make reading easier.

Level 3—for Second-Grade through Third-Grade Children
Level 3 books have considerably longer texts, harder words, and more complicated sentences.

All Aboard for happy reading!

To Cody, Carly, Evan, Justin,
and Morgan—M.B.

"To he who grows us up"—J.E.M.S.

Special thanks to Nancy Gibson, co-founder of the International Wolf
Center.

Text copyright © 1998 by Mary Batten. Illustrations copyright © 1998 by Jo Ellen
McAllister Stammen. All rights reserved. Published by Grosset & Dunlap, Inc., a member
of Penguin Putnam Books for Young Readers, New York. ALL ABOARD READING
is a trademark of The Putnam & Grosset Group. GROSSET & DUNLAP is a trademark
of Grosset & Dunlap, Inc. Published simultaneously in Canada. Printed in the U.S.A.

Library of Congress Cataloging-in-Publication

Batten, Mary.
    Baby wolf / by Mary Batten ; illustrated by Jo Ellen McAllister Stammen.
        p.   cm.—(All aboard reading. Level 2)
    Summary : Describes how a wolf pup grows through its first year with its siblings and other
members of its pack.
    1. Wolves—Infancy—Juvenile literature. 2. Wolves—Behavior—Juvenile literature.
3. Parental behavior in animals—Juvenile literature. [1. Wolves. 2. Animals—Infancy.]
I. McAllister Stammen, Jo Ellen, ill. II. Title. III. Series.
QL737.C22B375 1998
599.773—dc21   97-29413
                                                                                            CIP
ISBN 0-448-41833-9 (GB)   A B C D E F G H I J   AC
ISBN 0-448-41645-X (pbk)   A B C D E F G H I J

ALL
ABOARD
READING™

Level 2
Grades 1-3

Baby Wolf

By Mary Batten

Illustrated by
Jo Ellen McAllister Stammen

Grosset & Dunlap • New York

Underground in a warm den,
a baby gray wolf is born.
The mother gray wolf licks
the pup to clean her.

Soon another pup is born.

Then another and another.

There are four babies in all.

The babies crawl over each other.

They drink their mother's

warm milk.

They cannot hear or see yet.

For now, all they do

is eat and sleep.

Outside, it is spring on their island home.

For the first few weeks,

the father wolf brings food to the mother.

She needs to stay inside the den

with her babies.

The father and mother

are the leaders of the whole wolf pack.

This pack is lucky.

No hunting is allowed here

on the island.

One sunny morning,

the baby wolves go outside the den

for the first time.

Everything is new to them.

The baby wolf feels the heat of the sun.

She sees the tall trees and the sky.

She plays in the grass
with her sister and brothers.

They look and act like dog puppies.

That is not surprising.

Wolves and dogs are part
of the same animal family.

The baby wolf is eight weeks old now.

She no longer drinks her mother's milk.

She sniffs and licks at the mouth

of an adult wolf.

This is how she asks for food.

The adult spits up some food

for the little wolf.

This may not sound good to you.

But it is perfect food

for a growing wolf pup.

All the adult wolves help feed
and take care of the babies.
The fifteen wolves in the pack
are all one family.

One day in early summer,

the baby wolf smells something new.

It is not her mother.

It is not her father,

or any other wolf.

The other wolves smell it, too.

Right away their ears

and tails stand up.

It is a large black bear

and her cubs!

The baby wolf hides behind a rock

with her sister and brothers.

Her father, mother,

and two other wolves rush to attack.

They show their sharp teeth.

They bark and growl.

At first, the bears stand still.

They do not want a fight.

Then slowly they move away.

All the wolf pups come out

from behind the rock.

They are safe!

The baby wolves are growing up fast.

They have left their den for good.

Now, they stay outside

and sleep with the adults.

Sometimes one pup climbs
on top of another pup.
Just like the pack leaders do
to keep order.

The pups watch the adult wolves
and copy them.

They even try to hunt, too.

The baby wolf spots a mouse.

Off she goes after it.

She chases it under a log.

This time the mouse gets away.

But one day,

the baby wolf will be a great hunter

like her mother and father.

AuOOOhoooooooooo.

The baby wolf

and her brothers and sister

learn to howl, too.

Howling is wolf talk.

It calls the pack together.

First one wolf howls.

Then others join in.

They wag their tails.

They act as if they are singing

a happy song.

Often wolves howl

before they go hunting.

Summer turns to fall.

The weather gets colder.

By late October, the first snow falls.

The pups are only six months old.

But they look almost grown up.

Their puppy teeth are gone.

Now they have big teeth

and thick coats to keep them warm.

Wolves need a lot of space
to live and hunt.
Sometimes the pack travels
many miles in a day.

Usually wolves hunt at night.
It is easier to sneak up
on other animals in the dark.
The pack members work together
to kill a big animal like a moose.

Wolves do not find food

every time they hunt.

So when they kill a moose or deer,

they eat a lot.

Each wolf can eat

as much as twenty pounds of meat

in one meal.

You would have to eat eighty large

hamburgers to eat that much!

By the end of winter,

the baby wolf is almost a year old.

She is not a baby anymore.

She knows her father and mother

are the leaders of the pack.

Like the other wolves,

she holds her tail low

or lies on the ground

when they are nearby.

Each wolf knows its place

in the pack.

In the spring,

the young wolf and the pack

go back to the place

where she was born.

Soon her mother will give birth
to new baby wolves.
And next year, the young wolf
may have babies of her own.

Now it is night.

The moon is high in the sky.

The wolves get ready

for their hunt.

The young wolf

takes her place in the pack.

Her father raises his head

and begins to howl.

AuOOOhooooooooo.

The other wolves join in.

AuOOOhooooooooo.

AuOOOhooooooooo.

"We are wolves.

We are here."